A Gift Book from Robert Frederick • The Fairy Tale Collection • A Gift Book from Robert Frederick • The Fairy Tale Collection • A Gift Book from Robert Frederick • The Fairy Tale Collection • A Gift Book from Robert Frederick • The Fairy Tale Collection • A Gift Book from Robert Frederick • The Fairy Tale Collection • A Gift Book from Robert Frederick • The Fairy Tale Collection • A Gift Book from Robert Frederick • The Fairy Tale Collection • A Gift Book from Robert Frederick • The Fairy Tale Collection • A Gift Book from Robert Frederick • The Fairy Tale Collection • A Gift Book from Robert Frederick • The Fairy Tale Collection • A Gift Book from Robert Frederick • The Fairy Tale Collection • A Gift Book from Robert Frederick • The Fairy Tale Collection • A Gift Book from Robert Frederick • The Fairy Tale Collection • A Gift Book from Robert Frederick • The Fairy Tale Collection • A Gift Book from Robert Frederick • The Fairy Tale Collection • A Gift Book from Robert Frederick • The Fairy Tale Collection • A Gift Book from Robert Frederick • The Fairy Tale Collection • A Gift Book from Robert Frederick • The Fairy Tale Collection • A Gift Book from Robert Frederick • The Fairy Tale Collection • A Gift Book from Robert Frederick • The Fairy Tale Collection

Acknowledgements:
Illustrated by Charles Robinson
Edited by Walter Jerrold
Printed in Malaysia

My Book of
Fairy Tales

Volume 4

INTRODUCTION

ALL the best fairy-tales seem to be the old ones. The stories that entranced the childhood of our parents are still the favourites, though the manner of their telling has altered. Further, it may be said that the best nursery tales are told in a universal language. If only his story is worthy, it ensures the teller the freedom of the nursery everywhere.

Could the story-tellers represented in this volume be assembled to lead, in a Grand Nursery Pageant, their Princes and Princesses, Ogres and

INTRODUCTION

Fairies, what a varied spectacle it would be! Perhaps the place of honour would be given to the old Oriental who collected the tales of the *Arabian Nights*, and who would bring with him the far-travelled Sindbad. They would be followed by a Frenchman, Charles Perrault, with a delightful group including Blue Beard, Beauty, and the Beast. Dear Hans Andersen would present the Ugly Duckling and the Little Tin Soldier, and our own Robert Southey would have his hands full in charge of the Three Bears. As for Cinderella and Rumpelstiltskin, it would be hard to decide who should escort them, for under different names they play their part in the nursery romances of several countries.

Besides the celebrities would be strangers whose very names are unknown to us, but with whom we have long wanted to be friends. Amongst such anonymous authors we should see the story-tellers to whom we owe the histories of Dick Whittington and of the two famous Jacks—the Giant Killer and the proprietor of the Beanstalk.

What a welcome they would have wherever there are children, and grown-ups who have kept a young corner in their hearts!

These story-tellers are the true magicians: they can open the door between the nursery and fairyland.

CONTENTS

Hansel and Grethel

NCE as a poor woodman went to cut wood in the forest he heard a little cry; so he followed the sound, till at last he looked up a tree, and on one of the branches sat a tiny child. Its mother had fallen asleep, and a vulture had taken it out of her lap and flown away with it, and left it on the tree. The woodcutter climbed up, took the child down, and found it was a pretty little girl; and he said to himself: "I will take this child home, and bring her up with my son Hansel." So he brought her to his cottage, and called her Grethel, and the two children were so fond of each other that they were never happy except when together.

But the woodcutter became very poor, and had nothing in the world he could call his own; indeed he had scarcely

bread enough for his wife and the two children to eat. At last the time came when even that was all gone, and he knew not where to seek help in his need. At night, his wife said to him: " Husband, listen to me, and take the two children out early to-morrow morning; give each of them a piece of bread, and then lead them into the midst of the wood, where it is thickest, make a fire for them, and go away and leave them to shift for themselves, for we can no longer keep them here." And she would not let him have any peace until he came into her hard-hearted plan.

Meantime the poor children, lying awake restless, and weak from hunger, heard all that Hansel's mother said to her husband. "Now," thought Grethel to herself, "it is all up with us", and she began to weep. But Hansel crept to her bedside, and said: "Do not be afraid, Grethel, I will find some help for us." Then he got up, put on his jacket, and opened the door and went out.

The moon shone upon the little court before the cottage, and the white pebbles glittered like daisies on the meadows. So he stooped down, and put as many as he could into his pocket, and then went back to the house. "Now, Grethel," said he, "rest in peace!" and he went to bed and fell fast asleep.

HANSEL AND GRETHEL

Early in the morning the woodman's wife came and awoke them. "Get up, children," said she, "we are going into the wood; there is a piece of bread for each of you, but take care of it, and keep some for the afternoon."

Grethel took the bread, and carried it in her apron, because Hansel had his pocket full of stones; and they made their way into the wood.

After a time, Hansel stood still and looked towards home; and after a while he turned again, and so on several times. Then his father said: "Hansel, why do you keep turning and lagging about so?"

"Ah, Father," answered Hansel, "I am stopping to look

at my white cat, that sits on the roof, and wants to say goodbye to me."

"You little fool!" said his mother; "that is not your cat; it is the morning sun shining on the chimney-top."

Now Hansel had not been looking at the cat, but had all the while been lingering behind to drop from his pocket one white pebble after another along the road.

When they came into the midst of the wood, the woodman said: "Run about, children, and pick up some wood, and I will make a fire to keep us warm."

So they piled up a heap of brushwood, and set it on fire; and the mother said: "Now set yourselves by the fire, and go to sleep, while we go and cut wood in the forest. Be sure you wait till we come and fetch you." Hansel and Grethel sat by the fireside till the afternoon, and then ate their pieces of bread. They fancied the woodman was still in the wood, because they thought they heard the blows of his axe; but it was a bough which he had cunningly hung in such a way that the wind blew it against the other boughs; and so it sounded as the axe does in cutting. They waited till evening; but the woodman and his wife kept away, and no one came to fetch them.

When it was dark, Grethel began to cry; but Hansel said: "Wait till the moon rises." And when the moon rose he took her by the hand, and there lay the pebbles along the ground, glittering like new pieces of money, and marking out the way. Towards morning they came again to the woodman's house, and he was glad in his heart when he saw the children, for he had grieved at leaving them alone.

Not long afterwards there was again no bread in the house, and Hansel and Grethel heard the wife say to her husband: "The children found their way back once, and I took it in good part; but now there is only half a loaf of bread left for them in the house; to-morrow you must take them deeper into the wood, that they may not find their way out, or we shall be starved."

It grieved the husband in his heart to do as his selfish wife wished, and he thought it would be better to share their last morsel with the children; but, as he had done as she said once, he did not dare now to say no. When the children heard their plan, Hansel got up, and wanted to pick up pebbles as before. But when he came to the door, he found his mother had locked it. Still he comforted Grethel, and said: "Sleep in peace, dear Grethel! God is very kind, and will help us."

Early in the morning, a piece of bread was given to each of them, but smaller than the one they had before.

Upon the road Hansel crumbled his in his pocket, and often stood still and threw a crumb upon the ground. "Why do you lag so behind, Hansel?" said the woodman; "go your ways on before."

"I am looking at my little dove that is sitting upon the roof, and wants to say goodbye to me."

"You silly boy!" said the wife; "that is not your little dove; it is the morning sun, that shines on the chimney-top."

But Hansel went on crumbling his bread, and throwing it on the ground. And thus they went on farther into the wood.

There they were again told to sit down by a large fire, and go to sleep; and the woodman and his wife said they would come in the evening and fetch them away. In the afternoon, Hansel shared Grethel's bread, because he had strewed all his upon the road; but the day passed away, and evening passed away, and no one came to the poor children. Still Hansel comforted Grethel and said: "Wait till the moon rises; and then I shall be able to see the crumbs of bread which I have strewed, and they will show us the way home."

The moon rose; but when Hansel looked for the crumbs they were gone, for hundreds of little birds in the wood had found them and picked them up. Hansel, however, set out to try and find his way home; but they soon lost themselves, and went on through the night and all the next day, till at last they lay down and fell asleep. Another day they went on as before, but still did not come to the end of the wood; and they were as hungry as could be, for they had had nothing to eat.

In the afternoon of the third day they came to a strange

little hut, made of bread, with roof of cake, and windows of barley-sugar. "Now we will sit down and eat till we have had enough," said Hansel; "I will eat off the roof for my share; do you eat the windows, Grethel; they will be nice and sweet for you." Whilst Grethel, however, was picking at the barley-sugar, a pretty voice called softly from within:

"Tip, tap! who goes there?"

But the children answered:

"The wind, the wind,
That blows through the air!"

and went on eating. Now Grethel had broken out a round pane of the window for herself, and Hansel had torn off a large piece of cake from the roof, when the door opened, and a little old fairy came out. At this Hansel and Grethel were so frightened that they let fall what they had in their hands. But the old lady nodded to

them, and said: "Dear children, come in with me; you shall have something good."

So she led them into her little hut, and brought plenty to eat— milk and pancakes, with sugar, apples, and nuts; and then two beautiful little beds were got ready, and Grethel and Hansel laid themselves down, and thought they were in heaven. But the fairy was a spiteful one, and made her pretty sweetmeat house to entrap little children. Early in the morning she went to their little beds; and though she saw the two sleeping, and looking so sweetly, she had no pity on them, but was glad they were in her power. Then she took up Hansel, and fastened him in a coop by himself, and when he awoke he found himself behind a grating, shut up safely, as chickens are; but she shook Grethel, and called out: "Get up, you lazy little thing, and fetch some water; and go into the kitchen, and cook something good to eat. Your brother is shut up yonder. I shall fatten him, and when he is fat, I think I shall eat him."

When the fairy was gone, poor Grethel watched her time,

and got up, and ran to Hansel, and told him what she had heard, and said: "We must run away quickly, for the old woman is a bad fairy, and will kill us."

But Hansel said: "You must first steal away her fairy wand, that we may save ourselves if she should follow; and bring the pipe, too, that hangs up in her room."

Then the little maiden ran back, and fetched the magic wand and the pipe, and away they went together. So when the old fairy came back, and could see no one at home, she sprang in a great rage to the window, and looked out into the wide world (which she could do, far and near), and a long way off she spied Grethel, running away with her dear Hansel. "You are already a great way off," said she; "but you will still fall into my hands."

Then she put on her boots, which walked several miles at a step, and scarcely made two steps with them before she overtook the children; but Grethel saw that the fairy was coming after them, and, by the help of the wand, turned her friend Hansel into a lake of water, and herself into a swan, which swam about in the middle of it. So the fairy sat herself down on the shore, and took a great deal of trouble to decoy the swan, and threw crumbs of bread to it; but it would not come, and she was forced to go home in the evening without taking her revenge. Then Grethel changed herself and Hansel back into their own forms, and they journeyed on until the dawn; and then the maiden turned herself into a beautiful rose, that grew in the midst of a quickset hedge; and Hansel sat by the side.

The fairy soon came striding along. "Good piper," said she, "may I pluck yon beautiful rose for myself?"

"Oh yes!" answered he. "And then," thought he to

himself, "I will play you a tune meantime." So when she had crept into the hedge in a great hurry, to gather the flower—for she well knew what it was—he pulled out the pipe slily, and began to play. Now the pipe was a fairy pipe, and, whether they liked it or not, whoever heard it was obliged to dance. So the old fairy was forced to dance a merry jig, on and on, without any rest, and without being able to reach the rose. And as he did not cease playing a moment, the thorns at length tore the clothes from off her body, and pricked her sorely, and there she stuck quite fast.

Then Grethel set herself free, and on they went; but she grew tired, and Hansel said: "Now I will hasten home for help."

And Grethel said: "I will stay here in the meantime, and wait for you." Then Hansel went away.

But when Grethel had stayed in the field a long time, and found he did not come back, she became quite sorrowful, and turned herself into a little daisy, and thought to herself: "Someone will come and tread me under foot, and so my sorrows will end." But it so happened that, as a shepherd was keeping watch in a field, he saw the daisy; and, thinking it very pretty, he took it home, placed it in a box, and said: " I have never found so pretty a daisy before." From that time everything throve wonderfully at the shepherd's house. When he got up in the morning, all the household work was ready done: the room was swept and cleaned, the fire made, and the water fetched; and in the afternoon, when he came home, the cloth was laid, and a good dinner ready for him. Although it pleased him, he was at length troubled to think how it could be, and went to a cunning woman who lived hard by, and asked what he should do. She said: " There must be witchcraft in it. Look out to-morrow early, and see if anything stirs about in the room: if it does, throw a white cloth at once over it, and then the witchcraft will be stopped." The shepherd did as she said, and the next morning saw the box open, and the daisy come out; then he sprang up quickly, and threw a white cloth over it. In an instant the spell was broken, and Grethel stood before him, for it was she who had taken care of his house for him; and she was so beautiful that he asked her if she would marry him. She said " No", because she wished to be faithful to her dear Hansel; but she agreed to stay and keep house for him till Hansel came back.

Time passed on, and Hansel came back at last; for the spiteful fairy had led him astray, and he had not been able for a long time to find his way to Grethel. Then he and Grethel set out to go home; but, after travelling a long way, Grethel became tired, and she and Hansel laid themselves down to sleep in an old hollow tree. But as they slept, the fairy—who had got out of the bush at last—came by; and, finding her wand, was glad to lay hold of it, and at once turned poor Hansel into a fawn.

Soon Grethel awoke, and found what had happened. She wept bitterly over the poor creature; and the tears rolled down his eyes too, as he laid himself beside her. Then she said: "Rest in peace, dear fawn; I will never, never leave thee." So she took off her golden necklace, and put it round his neck, and plucked some rushes, and plaited them into a soft string to fasten to it, and led the poor little thing by her side when she went to walk in the wood; and when they were tired they came back, and lay down to sleep by the hollow tree; but nobody came near them except the little dwarfs that lived in the wood, and these watched over them.

At last one day they came to a cottage; and Grethel having looked in, and seen that it was empty, thought to herself: "We can stay and live here." Then she went and gathered leaves and moss to make a soft bed for the fawn; and every morning she went out and plucked nuts and berries for herself, and sweet shrubs and tender grass for her friend. In the evening, when Grethel was tired, she laid her head upon the fawn for her pillow, and slept; and if poor Hansel could but have his right form again, she thought they should lead a very happy life.

They lived a long while in the wood by themselves, till it chanced that the king of that country came hunting there. And when the fawn heard all around the echoing of the horns, and the baying of the dogs, and the merry shouts of the huntsmen, he wished very much to go and see what was going on. "Ah, sister," said he, "let me go out into the wood; I can stay no longer!" And he begged so long that she at last agreed to let him go. "But," said she, "be sure to come to me in the evening. I shall shut the door, to keep out those wild huntsmen, and if you tap at it and say: 'Sister, let me in!' I shall know you; but if you don't speak, I shall keep the door fast." Then away sprang the fawn. The king and his huntsmen saw the

beautiful creature, and followed but could not overtake him; for when they thought they were sure of their prize, he sprang over the bushes, and was out of sight.

As it grew dark he ran home to the hut and tapped, and said: "Sister, let me in!" Then she opened the door.

Next morning, when he heard the horn of the hunters, he said:

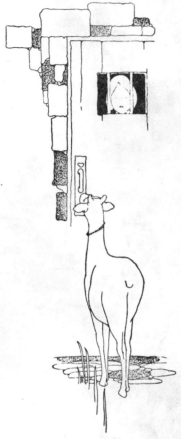

"Sister, open the door; I must go again." Then she said: "Come back in the evening, and remember what you are to say." When the king and the huntsmen saw the fawn with the golden collar again, they gave him chase; but he was too quick for them. The chase lasted the whole day; but at length the huntsmen nearly surrounded him, and one of them wounded him in the foot, so that he became sadly lame, and could hardly crawl home. The man who had wounded him followed close behind, and hid himself, and heard the little fawn say: "Sister, let me in!" upon which the door opened, and soon shut again. The huntsman went to the king and told him what he had seen and heard; then the king said: "To-morrow we will have another chase."

Grethel was frightened when she saw that her dear fawn was wounded; but she washed the blood away, and put some healing herbs on it, and said: "Now go to bed, dear fawn, and you will soon be well again." The wound was so slight that in the morning there was nothing to be seen of it; and when the horn blew, the little thing said: "I can't stay here; I must go and look on. I will take care that none of them shall catch me."

HANSEL AND GRETHEL

But Grethel said: "I am sure they will kill you this time: I will not let you go."

"I shall die of grief," said he, "if you keep me here. When I hear the horns, I feel as if I could fly."

Then Grethel was forced to let him go. So she opened the door with a heavy heart, and he bounded out.

When the king saw him, he said to his huntsmen: "Now chase him all day long, till you catch him; but let none of you do him any harm." The sun set, however, without their being able to overtake him, and the king called away the huntsmen, and said to the one who had watched: "Now come and show me the little hut." So they went to the door and tapped, and said: "Sister, let me in!" Then the door opened, and the king went in, and there stood a maiden more lovely than he had ever seen. Grethel was frightened to see that it was not her fawn, but a king with a golden crown, that was come into her hut; however, he spoke kindly to her, and took her hand, and said: "Will you come with me to my castle and be my wife?"

"Yes," said the maiden, "I will go to your castle, but I cannot be your wife; and my fawn must go with me. I cannot part with that."

"Well," said the king, "he shall come and live with you all your life, and want for nothing." Just then in sprang the fawn; and they left the hut in the wood together.

Then the king took Grethel to his palace, and on the way she told him all her story. And then he sent for the fairy, and made her change the fawn into Hansel again; and he and Grethel loved one another, and were married, and lived happily together all their days in the good king's palace.

Jack and the Beanstalk

JACK was the only son of a poor widow woman; he was a lazy and extravagant lad, and did not realize that he should have been working to support his mother instead of leaving her to work for him. At length they had nothing left but a cow, and the poor woman sent Jack to sell it at the neighbouring market.

As he was going along, Jack met a butcher who, finding he wished to sell the cow, offered in exchange for it a hatful of curious coloured beans. Jack thought this a fine bargain, and hurried home to his mother. The poor, disappointed woman upbraided him angrily, kicked the beans in a passion out of the cottage door, and they both went supperless to bed.

Early next morning Jack woke to find leaves shadowing his window. He ran downstairs, and saw that some of the beans had taken root and sprung up to a great height. The immense stalks had so entwined that they formed a ladder, the top of which seemed to be lost in the clouds.

JACK AND THE BEANSTALK

Jack set out climbing, and reached the top of the beanstalk quite exhausted. Looking around, he found himself in a strange, barren country, not a tree, shrub, house, or living thing to be seen. However, he walked on, hoping to see a house where he might beg something to eat and drink. Presently an infirm-looking woman approached: he saw that she was old and poor. She accosted Jack, enquiring how he came there; and he related the circumstances of the beanstalk. She then asked if he recollected his father. He replied he did not, and added there must be some mystery relating to him, for he had frequently asked his mother who his father was, but that she always burst into tears, and appeared violently agitated; nor did she recover herself for some days after. One thing he could not avoid observing upon those occasions, which was that she always carefully avoided answering him, and seemed afraid of speaking, as if there were some secret connected with his father's history. The old woman replied:

" I will reveal the whole story; your mother must not. But before I begin I require a solemn promise on your part to do what I command. I am a fairy, and if you do not perform exactly what I require, your mother and yourself shall both be destroyed."

Jack promised to fulfil her injunctions exactly, and the fairy continued:

" Your father, though only a private gentleman, was as rich as a prince, and deserved all he possessed, for he only lived to do good. There lived, a great many miles off, a giant who was altogether as wicked as your father was good; who was in his heart envious, covetous, and cruel; but who had the art of concealing those vices.

" Hearing of your father, he was determined to ingratiate himself into his favour. Your father credited the lying story he told, gave him handsome apartments in his own house, and caused him and his wife to be treated like visitors of consequence. Things went on in this way some time, the giant becoming daily more impatient to put his plan into execution. At last a favourable opportunity presented itself. Your father's house was at some distance from the seashore, but with a good glass the coast could be seen distinctly. The giant was one day using the telescope; the wind was very high; he saw a fleet of ships in distress off the rocks; he hastened to your father, mentioned this, and eagerly requested he would send all the servants he could spare to

relieve the sufferers. Everyone was instantly dispatched, except the porter and your nurse. The giant then joined your father in the study, and appeared to be delighted—he really was so. Your father recommended a favourite book, and was handing it down; the giant took the opportunity, and stabbed him; he instantly fell dead. The giant left the body, found the porter and nurse, and presently dispatched them. You were then only three months old. Your mother had you in her arms in a remote part of the house, and, ignorant of what was going on, went into the study. How was she shocked on discovering your father a corpse! She was stupefied with horror. The giant found her in that state, and hastened to serve her and you as he had done her husband; but she fell at his feet, and in a pathetic manner besought him to spare your life.

"The cruel giant for a short time was struck with remorse, and spared your lives; but first he made her swear solemnly that she never would inform you who your father was, or answer any questions concerning him, assuring her that if she did he would put both of you to death in the most cruel manner. Your mother took you in her arms and fled as quickly as possible. She was scarcely gone, when the giant repented that he had suffered her to escape: he would have pursued her instantly, but he had his own safety to provide for, as it was necessary he should be gone before the servants returned. He knew where to find all your father's treasure, soon loaded himself and his wife, set the house on fire in several places, and, when the servants returned, the house was burnt to the ground.

"Your poor mother, forlorn, abandoned, and forsaken, wandered with you many miles from this scene of desolation, and settled in the cottage where you were brought up; and it was owing to her fear of the giant that she has never mentioned your father to you.

"I became your father's guardian at his birth; but fairies have laws to which they are subject as well as mortals. A short time before the giant went to your father's, I transgressed; my punishment was a total suspension of power for a limited time—an unfortunate circumstance, as it prevented my succouring your father. The day on which you met the butcher, as you went to sell your mother's cow, my power was restored. It was I who secretly prompted you to take the beans in exchange for the cow. By my power the beanstalk grew to so great a height and formed a ladder. I need not add that I inspired you with a strong desire to ascend the ladder.

"The giant lives in this country. You are the person appointed to punish him for all his wickedness. You will have dangers and difficulties to encounter, but must persevere in avenging the death of your father, or you will always be miserable. As to the giant's possessions, you may seize all with impunity, for everything he has is yours, though now you are unjustly deprived of it. Go along the road; you will soon see the house where your cruel enemy lives. Remember the severe punishment that awaits you if you disobey my commands."

So saying, the fairy disappeared, leaving Jack to pursue his journey.

He walked until after sunset, and soon, to his great joy, spied a large mansion. A plain-looking woman was standing at the door. He accosted her, begging she would give him a morsel of bread and a night's lodging. She expressed great surprise on seeing him, said it was quite uncommon to see a human being near their house, for it was well known that her husband was a large and powerful giant, and that he would never eat anything but human flesh if he could possibly get it; that he did not think anything of walking fifty miles to procure it, usually being out all day for that purpose.

Jack hoped to elude the giant, and again entreated the woman to take him in for one night only, and hide him in the oven. The woman at last suffered herself to be persuaded, for she was of a compassionate disposition. She gave him plenty to eat and drink, and took him into the house.

A long gallery through which they passed was very dark, just light enough to show that, instead of a wall on one side, there was a grating of iron which parted off a dismal dungeon, whence issued the groans of poor victims whom the giant reserved in confinement for his own voracious appetite. Poor Jack was half-dead with fear, and gave himself up for lost. At the farther end of the gallery there

was a winding staircase, which led them into a spacious kitchen. A good fire was burning in the grate, and Jack, not seeing anything to make him uncomfortable, here forgot his fears, and was beginning to enjoy himself, when he was aroused by a loud knocking at the house door. The giant's wife ran to secure him in the oven, and then made what haste she could to let her husband in, and Jack heard him accost her in a voice like thunder, saying:

"Wife, I smell fresh meat."

"Oh, my dear," she replied, "it is nothing but the people in the dungeon!"

The giant appeared to believe her, and walked downstairs into the very kitchen where poor Jack was, who shook, trembled, and was more terrified than he had yet been. At last the monster seated himself by the fireside, whilst his wife prepared supper. By degrees Jack recovered himself sufficiently to look at the giant through a crevice. When supper was ended, the giant desired his wife to bring him his hen. A beautiful hen was brought, and placed upon the table. Jack observed that every time the giant said "Lay", the hen laid an egg of solid gold. The giant amused himself a long time with the hen; meanwhile his wife went to bed. At length the giant fell fast asleep by the fireside, and snored heavily.

At daybreak, Jack, finding the giant not likely to be soon roused, crept softly out of his hiding place, seized the hen, and ran off with her. He met with some difficulty in finding his way out of the house, but at last reached the road in safety, without fear of pursuit. He easily found the way to the beanstalk, and descended it better and quicker than he expected. His mother was overjoyed to see him.

"And now, Mother," said he, "I have brought home that which will quickly make you rich without any trouble. I hope I have made you some amends for the affliction I have caused you through my idleness, extravagance, and folly."

The hen produced them as many eggs as they desired; they sold them, and in a little time became very rich.

For some months Jack and his mother lived happily together; but he longed to climb the beanstalk, and pay the giant another visit, in order to carry off some more of his treasures. A few mornings later he rose very early, put on a disguise, and, unperceived by anyone, climbed the beanstalk. He was greatly fatigued when he reached the top, and very hungry. He reached the giant's castle late in the evening; the woman was standing at the door as usual. Jack accosted her, at the same time telling her a pitiful tale, and requested that she would give him victuals and drink, and a night's lodging. She told him what he knew before, concerning her husband, and also that she one night admitted a poor, hungry, distressed boy, who was half-dead with travelling; that he stole one of the giant's treasures;

and ever since that her husband was worse than before, and used her very cruelly, upbraiding her continually with being the cause of his loss. Jack did his best to persuade the woman to admit him, and found it a very hard task; but at last she consented, and, as she led the way, Jack observed that everything was just as before. She took him into the kitchen, and hid him in an old lumber closet. The giant returned at the usual time, and walked in so heavily that the house was shaken to the foundation. He seated himself by the fire, saying:

" I smell fresh meat!"

The wife replied that it was the crows, who had brought a piece of carrion, and laid it at the top of the house upon the leads.

While supper was preparing, the giant was very ill-tempered and impatient, frequently lifting up his hand to strike his wife for not being quick enough. She, however, was always so fortunate as to elude the blow. He was also continually upbraiding her with the loss of his hen. Then, having eaten till he was quite satisfied, he said to his wife:

" I must have something to amuse me, either my bags of money or my harp."

After a great deal of ill humour, and having teased his wife some time, he commanded her to bring his bags of gold and silver. Jack, as before, peeped out, and presently the woman brought two bags into the room; they were of an immense size—one filled with new guineas, the other with new shillings. They were placed before the giant: he reprimanded his wife most severely for staying so long. The poor woman replied, trembling with fear, that they were so heavy she could scarcely lift them, and that she had nearly

24

fainted owing to their weight. This so exasperated the giant that he raised his hand to strike her. She, however, escaped, and went to bed, leaving him to count over his treasures by way of amusement.

First the bag containing the silver was emptied, and the contents placed upon the table. Jack viewed the glittering heaps with delight, and heartily wished the contents in his own possession. The giant reckoned the silver over and over again, then put it all carefully into the bag, which he made secure. The other bag was opened next, and the guineas placed upon the table. If Jack was pleased at the sight of the silver, he felt much more de- lighted when he saw such a heap of gold. The gold was put up as the silver had been before, and, if possible, more securely. The giant snored aloud; Jack could compare his noise to nothing but the roaring of the sea in a high wind when the tide is coming in. At last, conclud- ing him to be asleep, and therefore secure, Jack stole out of his hiding place, and approached in order to carry off the two bags of money. Just as he laid his hand upon one of them, a little dog started out from under the giant's chair, and barked most furiously, so that Jack gave himself up for lost. Fear riveted him to the spot; instead of running,

he stood still, expecting his enemy to awake every moment; but the giant continued in sleep, and the dog grew weary of barking. Jack looked round, saw a large piece of meat, which he threw to the dog, who took it into the lumber closet which Jack had just left.

He found himself thus delivered from a noisy and troublesome enemy; and, as the giant did not awake, Jack seized both the bags, and carried them away. He reached the house door in safety, and found it quite daylight. The only difficulty he had arose from the weight of the bags, and they were so heavy he could hardly carry them. Jack was overjoyed when he found himself near the beanstalk; he soon reached the bottom, and immediately ran to seek his mother. An old woman said she was at a neighbour's, ill of a fever, and directed him to the house where she was. He was shocked on finding her apparently dying, and could scarcely bear his own reflections on knowing himself to be the cause. On being told of his return, she began to recover gradually. Jack presented her with his two bags, and they lived happily and comfortably for some time. Notwithstanding the comfort, Jack's mind dwelt upon the beanstalk; he could not think of anything else. His mother found that

something preyed upon his mind, and endeavoured to discover what it was; but Jack knew too well what the consequence would be of disclosing the cause of his melancholy.
He did his utmost to conquer the great desire he felt for
another journey. However, finding the inclination grow too
powerful for him, he began to make secret preparations; and,
on the longest day, arose as soon as it was light, ascended
the beanstalk, and reached the top with some trouble. He
found the road and journey much as before.

He arrived at the giant's mansion late in the
evening, and found the wife standing at the
door. Jack had disguised himself so com-
pletely that she did not appear to have the
least recollection of him. How-
ever, when he pleaded hunger
and poverty in order to gain
admittance, he found it very
difficult indeed to persuade
her. At last he prevailed, and
was concealed in the copper.
When the giant returned in
the evening, he said:

"I smell fresh meat!"

Jack felt quite composed,
as he had said so before, and
was soon satisfied; however,
the giant started up suddenly,
and, notwithstanding all his
wife could say, searched all
around the room. Whilst
this was going on, Jack was

ready to die with fear; and when the giant approached the copper, and even put his hand upon the lid, Jack thought his death warrant was signed. But fortunately the giant ended his search there, without moving the lid of the copper, and seated himself quietly by the table. This fright nearly overcame poor Jack; he was afraid of moving or even breathing, lest he should be heard and captured.

The giant at last ate a great supper. When he had finished his meal he commanded his wife to fetch his harp. Jack peeped under the copper lid, and saw the most wonderful and beautiful harp that could be imagined. The giant said "Play", and it instantly played without being touched. The music was very fine; Jack was delighted, for he had never heard anything like it before, and felt more anxious to get the magic harp into his possession than either of the former treasures. The sweet music lulled the giant into a sound sleep, and the woman went into the back-kitchen. Jack quickly made up his mind, got out of the copper, and took the harp. But the harp, however, was a fairy, and called out loudly: "Master! master! master!"

The giant awoke, stood up, and tried to pursue Jack, but he had drunk so much wine that he could not stand Poor Jack ran as fast as he could.

In a little time the giant was sufficiently recovered to walk slowly, or rather to reel, after him; had he been sober he must have overtaken Jack instantly; but, as he then was, Jack contrived to be the first at the top of the beanstalk. The giant, roaring with anger, and calling to him all the way, was sometimes very near him.

The moment Jack set his foot on the beanstalk he

called at the top of his voice for a hatchet. One was brought directly. He soon reached the ground. Just at that instant the giant was beginning to come down; but Jack, with his hatchet, cut the beanstalk close off to the root,

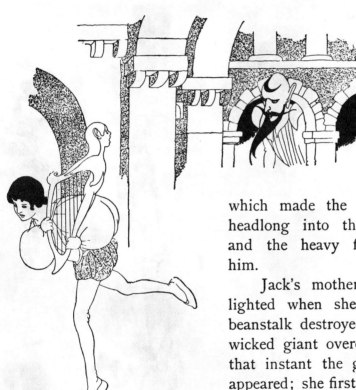

which made the giant fall headlong into the garden, and the heavy fall killed him.

Jack's mother was delighted when she saw the beanstalk destroyed and the wicked giant overcome. At that instant the good fairy appeared; she first addressed Jack's mother, and explained every circumstance relating to the journeys up the great beanstalk. The fairy then charged Jack to be a dutiful and affectionate son to his mother, and to follow his father's good example in everything, which was the only way to be respectable and happy in this life. After giving this advice she took her leave of them and disappeared from their sight. Jack humbly and with his whole heart begged his mother's pardon for all the sorrow and affliction he had caused her, promising faithfully to be very dutiful and obedient to her for the future. He proved as good as his word, and was a pattern of affectionate behaviour and attention to parents. His mother and he lived together a great many years, and continued to be always very happy.

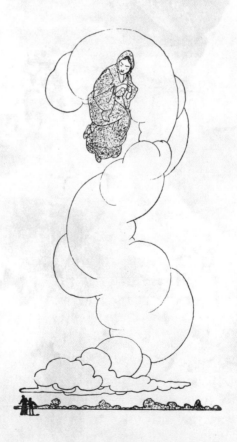

Little Chicken Kluk

HERE was once a little chicken called Kluk. A nut fell on his back, and gave him such a blow that he rolled on the ground. So he ran to the hen, and said: "Henny Penny, run, I think all the world is falling!"

"Who has told thee that, little chicken Kluk?"

"Oh, a nut fell on my back, and struck me so that I rolled on the ground."

"Then let us run," said the hen.

So they ran to the cock, and said: "Cocky Locky, run, I think all the world is falling."

"Who has told thee that, Henny Penny?"

"Little chicken Kluk."

"Who told thee that, little chicken Kluk?"

"Oh, a nut fell on my back, and struck me so that I rolled on the ground."

"Then let us run," said the cock.

So they ran to the duck, and said: "Ducky Lucky, run, I think all the world is falling."

"Who told thee that, Cocky Locky?"

"Henny Penny."

31

"Who has told thee that, Henny Penny?"

"Little chicken Kluk."

"Who has told thee that, little chicken Kluk?"

"Oh, a nut fell on my back, and struck me so that I rolled on the ground."

"Then let us run," said the duck.

So they ran to the goose, and said: "Goosy Poosy, run, I think all the world is falling."

"Who has told thee that, Ducky Lucky?"

"Cocky Locky."

"Who has told thee that, Cocky Locky?"

"Henny Penny."

"Who has told thee that, Henny Penny?"

"Little chicken Kluk."

"Who has told thee that, little chicken Kluk?"

"Oh, a nut fell on my back, and struck me so that I rolled on the ground."

"Then let us run," said the goose.

Then they ran to the fox, and said: "Foxy Coxy, run, I think all the world is falling."

"Who has told thee that, Goosy Poosy?"

"Ducky Lucky."

"Who has told thee that, Ducky Lucky?"

"Cocky Locky."

"Who has told thee that, Cocky Locky?"

"Henny Penny."

"Who has told thee that, Henny Penny?"

"Little chicken Kluk."

"Who has told thee that, little chicken Kluk?"

"Oh, a nut fell on my back, and struck me so that I rolled on the ground."

C 165

"SO THEY ALL RAN INTO THE WOOD"

33

"Then let us run," said the fox.

So they all ran into the wood. Then the fox said: "I must now count and see if I have got you all here. I, Foxy Coxy, one; Goosy Poosy, two; Ducky Lucky, three; Cocky Locky, four; Henny Penny, five; and little chicken Kluk, six; Hei! that one I'll snap up." He then said "Let us run."

So they ran farther into the wood. Then said he: "Now I must count and see if I have got you all here. I, Foxy Coxy, one; Goosy Poosy, two; Ducky Lucky, three; Cocky Locky, four; Henny Penny, five; Hei! that one I'll snap up."

And so he went on till he had eaten them all up.

The Little Match Girl

T was the last evening of the year. In the cold and darkness a poor little girl, with bare head and feet, was wandering about the streets, her feet quite red and blue with the cold. In her tattered apron she carried a bundle of matches, and there were a good many more in her hand. No one had bought any of them the livelong day—no one had given her a single penny. Trembling with cold and hunger, she crept on, the picture of sorrow.

The snowflakes settled on her long, fair hair, which fell in ringlets over her shoulders; but she thought neither of her own beauty, nor of the cold. Lights shone from every window, and the smell of roast goose reached her, for it was New Year's eve, and it was of that she thought.

In a corner formed by two houses, one of which came a little farther forward than the other, she sat down, drawing her feet close under her, but in vain—she could not warm them. She dared not go home—she had sold no matches, earned not a single penny, and her father would certainly beat her; besides, her home was almost as cold as the street —it was an attic; and, although the larger of the many holes in the roof were stopped up with straw and rags, the cold wind came whistling through. Her hands were nearly frozen. A match would warm them, perhaps, if she dared light it. She drew one out, and struck it against the wall. It was a bright, warm light, like a little candle, and she held her hands over it. It was quite a wonderful light. It seemed to that poor little girl as though she were sitting before a large iron stove with polished brass feet and brass ornaments. So beautifully did the fire within burn that the child stretched out her feet to warm them also. Alas! in an instant the flame had died away, the stove vanished, and the little girl sat cold and comfortless, with the remains of the burnt match in her hand.

A second match was struck; it kindled and blazed, and wherever its light fell the wall became transparent as a veil, and the little girl could see into the room. She saw the table spread with a snowy-white tablecloth and set with shining china dinner dishes. A roast goose, stuffed with apples and dried plums, stood at one

end, smoking hot, and—pleasantest of all to see—the goose, with knife and fork still in her breast, jumped down from the dish, and waddled along the floor right up to the poor child. The match was burnt out, and only the thick, hard wall was beside her.

She lighted a third match. Again the flame shot up, and now she was sitting under a most beautiful Christmas-tree, far larger, and far more prettily decked out than the one

she had seen last Christmas-eve through the glass doors of the rich merchant's house. Thousands of wax tapers lighted up the branches, and tiny painted figures, such as she had seen in the shop windows, looked down from the tree upon her. The child stretched out her hands towards them and the match went out. Still, however, the Christmas candles burned higher and higher, till they looked to her like the stars in the sky. One of them fell, the light streaming behind it like a long, fiery tail.

"Now someone is dying," said the little girl softly, for she had been told by her old grandmother, the only person who had ever been kind to her—but she was now dead,—that whenever a star falls a soul flies up to God. She struck another match against the wall and the light shone round her, and in its brightness she saw her dear dead grandmother, gentle and loving as always, but bright and happy as she had never looked during her lifetime.

"Grandmother!" said the child, "oh, take me with you! I know you will leave me as soon as the match goes out—you will vanish like the warm stove, like the New Year's feast, and like the beautiful Christmas-tree." And she hastily lighted all the remaining matches in the bundle, lest her grandmother should disappear. And the matches burned with such a splendour, that noonday could scarcely have been brighter. Never had the good old grandmother looked so tall and stately, so beautiful and kind. She took the little girl in her arms, and they both flew away together radiant with happiness. They flew far above the earth higher and higher, till they were in that place where neither cold, nor hunger, nor pain is ever known,—in the presence of God.

But in the cold morning hour, crouching in the corner of

the wall, the poor little girl was found—her cheeks glowing, her lips smiling—frozen to death on the last night of the Old Year. The New Year's sun shone on the lifeless child; motionless she sat there with the matches in her lap, one bundle of them quite burnt out.

"She has been trying to warm herself, poor thing!" some people said; but no one knew of the sweet visions she had beheld, or how gloriously she and her grandmother were celebrating their New Year's festival.

Beauty and the Beast

THERE was once a merchant who had six children, three boys and three girls. The three daughters were all handsome, but particularly the youngest; so very beautiful indeed was she, that everyone, during her childhood, called her the Little Beauty, and being still the same when she was grown up, nobody called her by any other name; which made her sisters extremely jealous. This youngest daughter was not only handsomer than her sisters, but was better tempered also.

Owing to some accident the merchant suddenly lost his fortune, having nothing left but a small cottage in the country. He said to his daughters, the tears all the time running down his cheeks:

" My children, we must go and live in the cottage, and try

to get a subsistence by labour, for we have no other means of support left!"

When they had removed to their cottage, the merchant and his three sons employed themselves in the fields and garden, that they might have corn and vegetables for their support. Beauty rose by four o'clock, lighted the fires, cleaned the house, and got the breakfast for the whole family. When she had done her work she amused herself with reading, playing on the harpsichord, or singing as she spun. Her sisters were at a loss what to do to pass the time away! they breakfasted in bed, and did not rise till ten, when they walked out, but finding themselves very soon tired, would frequently sit down under a shady tree, and lament the loss of their carriage and fine clothes.

The family had lived in this manner about a year, when the merchant received a letter, which informed him that one of his richest vessels, which he thought lost, had arrived in port. This made the two sisters almost mad with joy. When they found it necessary for their father to take a journey to the ship they begged he would bring them on his return some new gowns, caps, rings, and all sorts of trinkets. Beauty asked for nothing; for she thought that the ship's cargo would scarcely purchase all that her sisters wished for.

"You, Beauty," said the merchant, "ask for nothing; what can I bring you?"

"Since you are so kind as to think of me, dear father," answered she, "I should be obliged to you to bring me a rose, for we have none in our garden."

It was not that Beauty wished for a rose, but she was unwilling to condemn, by her example, the conduct of her sisters, who would have said she refused only to be praised. The merchant took his leave, and set out on his journey; but, on arriving at the port, some dishonest persons went to law with him about the merchandise; so after a great deal of trouble he returned to his cottage as poor as he had left it. When he was within thirty miles of his home, and thinking of the happiness he should enjoy in again embracing his children, his road lay through a thick forest, and he lost himself. All at once, happening to look down a long avenue, he discovered a light, but it seemed at a great distance. He pursued his way towards it, and found it proceeded from a splendid palace brilliantly illuminated. He quicked his pace, and was surprised to find not a single creature in any of the outer yards. His horse, which followed him, finding a stable with the door open, entered, and, being nearly starved, helped himself to a plentiful meal of oats and hay. His master then tied him up, and walked towards the house, which he entered, without, to his great astonishment, seeing a living creature: pursued his way to a large hall, in which was a good fire, and a table provided with the most delicate dishes, on which was laid a single cover.

As snow and rain had wetted him to the skin, he approached the fire.

"I hope," says he, "the master of the house or his servants will excuse the liberty I take, for it surely will not be long before they make their appearance."

He waited a considerable time, and still nobody came: at length the clock struck eleven; and the merchant, overcome with hunger and thirst, helped himself to a chicken, of which he made but two mouthfuls, and then to a few glasses of wine, all the time trembling with fear. He sat till the clock struck twelve, and not a creature had he seen. He now took courage, and began to think of looking a little farther about him: accordingly, he opened a door at the end of the hall, and entered an apartment magnificently furnished, which opened into another, in which there was an excellent bed; and finding himself quite overcome with fatigue, he resolved to shut the door, undress, and get into it. It was ten o'clock the next morning before he thought of rising; when, what was his astonishment at seeing a handsome suit of clothes entirely new, in the place of his own, which were quite spoiled!

"No doubt," said he to himself, "this palace belongs to some good fairy, who has taken pity on my unfortunate situation."

He looked out of the window; and instead of snow, he saw the most delightful flowers. He returned to the hall where he had supped, and found a breakfast table, with chocolate ready prepared.

"Truly, my good fairy," said the merchant aloud, "I am extremely indebted to you for your kind care of me."

Having made a hearty breakfast, he took his hat, and was going toward the stable to pay his horse a visit. As he passed under one of the arbours, which was loaded with roses, he recollected Beauty's request, and gathered a bunch of them to carry home. At the same instant he heard a most horrible noise, and saw such a hideous Beast approaching him, that he was ready to sink with fear!

"Ungrateful man!" said the Beast in a terrible voice; "I have saved your life by receiving you in my palace, and in return you steal my roses, which I value more than all my other possessions. With your life you shall atone your fault: you shall die in a quarter of an hour!"

The merchant fell on his knees, and, clasping his hands, said:

"My lord, I humbly entreat your pardon: I did not think it could offend you to gather a rose for one of my daughters."

"I am not a lord, but a beast," replied the monster; "I do not like compliments, but that people should say what they think; so do not imagine you can move me with your flattery. You say, however, that you have daughters; I will pardon you, on condition that one of them shall come hither and die in your

place: do not attempt to argue with me, but go; and if your daughters should refuse, swear to me that you will return in three months."

The merchant had no intention to let one of his daughters die in his stead; but thought that, by seeming to accept the Beast's condition, he should have the satisfaction of once again embracing them. He accordingly swore, and the Beast told him he might set off as soon as he pleased: "but," added he, "it is my will that you should not go empty-handed. Go back," continued he, "to the chamber in which you slept, where you will find an empty chest: fill it with whatever you like best, and I will get it conveyed to your own house."

The Beast then went away, and the good merchant said to himself:

"If I must die, yet I shall have the consolation of leaving my children some provision."

He returned to the chamber in which he had slept; and having found a great quantity of pieces of gold, filled the chest with them to the very brim, locked it, and, mounting his horse, left the palace. The horse of itself took a path across the forest, and in a few hours they reached the merchant's house. His children gathered round him as he dismounted, but the merchant, instead of embracing them with joy, could not, as he looked at them, refrain from weeping. He held in his hand the bunch of roses, which he gave to Beauty, saying:

"Take these roses, Beauty; little do you think how dear they have cost your unhappy father;" and then gave an account of all that had happened in the palace of the Beast. The two eldest sisters immediately began to shed tears, and to reproach Beauty, who they said would be the cause of her father's death.

"See," said they, "the consequence of the pride of the little wretch; why did she not ask for fine things as we did? But, forsooth, she must distinguish herself; and though she will be the cause of her father's death she does not shed a tear."

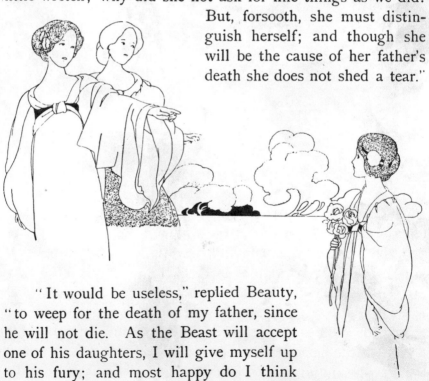

"It would be useless," replied Beauty, "to weep for the death of my father, since he will not die. As the Beast will accept one of his daughters, I will give myself up to his fury; and most happy do I think myself in being able at once to save his life, and prove my tenderness to the best of fathers."

" No, sister," said the three brothers, " you shall not die: we will go in search of this monster, and he or we will perish."

" Do not hope to kill him," said the merchant; " for his power is by far too great for this to be possible. I am charmed with the kindness of Beauty, but I will not suffer her life to be exposed. I am old, and cannot expect to live much longer: I shall therefore have lost but a few years of my life, which I regret only for my children's sake."

" Never, my father," cried Beauty, " shall you go to the palace without me; for you cannot prevent my following you: though young, I am not overfond of life, and I had much rather be devoured by the monster than die of the grief your loss would occasion me."

The merchant tried in vain to reason with Beauty, for she was determined to go. He was, indeed, so afflicted with the idea of losing his child, that he never thought of the chest filled with gold; but, retiring to his chamber at night, to his great surprise, perceived it standing by his bedside. He now determined to say nothing to his eldest daughters of the riches he possessed; for he knew very well they would immediately wish to return to town: but he told Beauty his secret, who informed him that two gentlemen had been visiting at their cottage during his absence, who had a great affection for her two sisters. She entreated her father to marry them without delay; for she was so sweet-tempered, that she loved them notwithstanding their unkind behaviour, which she forgave with all her heart.

When the three months had passed, the merchant and

THE BEAST

Beauty prepared to set out for the palace of the Beast; the two sisters rubbed their eyes with an onion, to make - believe they shed a great many tears: but both the mer-

chant and his sons shed them in reality. Beauty did not weep, for she thought this would only increase their affliction. They reached the palace in a few hours: when the horse, without bidding, entered the stable, and the merchant with his daughter proceeded to the large hall, where they found a table provided with every delicacy, and with two covers laid on it. The merchant had little appetite; but Beauty, the better to conceal her sorrow, placed herself at table, and, having helped her father, began to eat, thinking all the time, that the Beast had surely a mind to fatten her before he ate her up, since he had provided such good cheer. When they had finished their supper they heard a great noise; and the good old man began to bid his poor child farewell, for he knew it was the Beast coming to them. Beauty, on seeing his form, could not help being terrified, but tried as much as possible to conceal her fear. The monster asked her if she had come willingly; she replied, trembling still more:

"Y-e-s."

"You are a good girl," replied he, "and I think myself much obliged to you. Good man," continued he, "you may leave the palace to-morrow morning, and take care to return to it no more. Good-night, Beauty!"

"Good-night, Beast!" answered she; and the monster withdrew.

"Ah! dear child," said the merchant, embracing her, "I am half dead at the thoughts of your being sacrificed to this frightful monster: believe me, you had better go back, and let me stay."

"No," answered Beauty firmly, "to this I will never consent; you must go home to-morrow morning."

They now wished each other a sorrowful goodnight, and went to bed, thinking it would be impossible for them to close their eyes; but no sooner had they lain down, than they fell into a profound sleep, from which they did not awake till morning. Beauty dreamed that a lady approached her, who said:

"I am much pleased, Beauty, with the generous affection you have shown, in being willing to give your life to save that of your father; it shall not go unrewarded."

Beauty related this dream to her father; but though it afforded him some comfort, he could not take leave of his darling child without shedding bitter tears. When the merchant was out of sight, Beauty sat down in the large hall and began to cry also; but as she had a great deal of courage, she soon resolved not to make her unhappy condition still worse by useless sorrow. She determined on taking a view of the different parts of the palace, with which she was much delighted. What was her surprise, at coming to a door on which was written "Beauty's apartment"! She opened it hastily, and her eyes were dazzled by the splendour of everything it contained: but the things that more than all the rest excited her wonder, were a large library of books, a harpsichord, and music.

"The Beast is determined I shall not want amusement," said she. The thought then struck her, that it was not likely such provision should have been made for her, if she had but one day to live. She opened the library, and perceived a book, on which was written, in letters of gold:—

"Beauteous lady, dry your tears,
    Here's no cause for sighs or fears;
    Command as freely as you may,
    Compliance still shall mark your sway".

"Alas!" thought she, "there is nothing I so much desire

50

as to see my poor father, and to
know what he is this moment doing."

Great was her amazement, when,
casting her eyes on a looking-glass
that stood near, she saw her home,
and her father riding up to the cottage in the deepest affliction. Her
sisters had come out to meet him
who, notwithstanding all their
endeavours to look sorry, could
not help betraying their joy.
In a short time this disappeared; but
Beauty began
to think that
the Beast was
very kind to
her; and that
she had no-
thing to fear.
About noon
she found a
table pre-
pared, and a delightful concert of music played all the time
she was eating her dinner, without her seeing a single
creature. At supper, when she was going to place herself
at table, she heard the noise of the Beast, and could not
help trembling with terror.

"Will you allow me, Beauty," said he, "the pleasure of
seeing you sup?"

"That is as you please," answered she.

"Not in the least," said the Beast, "and the Beast you alone command in this place. If you dislike my company, you have only to say so, and I shall leave you. But tell me, Beauty, do you not think me very ugly?"

"Truly, yes," replied she, "for I cannot tell a falsehood; but I think you are very good."

"You are right," continued the Beast; "and, besides my ugliness, I am also ignorant; I know well enough that I am but a beast.

"Pray do not let me interrupt you eating," pursued he: "and be sure you do not want for anything, for all you see is yours, and I shall be grieved if you are not happy."

"You are very good," replied Beauty, "I must confess I think very highly of your disposition; and that makes me almost forget your ugliness."

"Yes, I trust I am good-tempered," said he, "but still I am a monster."

"Many men are more monsters than you," replied Beauty; "and I am better pleased with you in that form, ugly as it is, than with those who, under the form of men, conceal wicked hearts."

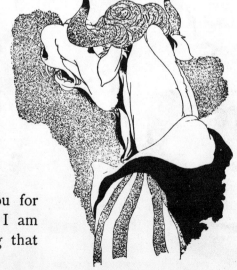

"If I had any understanding," resumed the Beast, "I would thank you for what you have said; but I am too stupid to say anything that could give you pleasure."

Beauty supped with an excellent appetite, and had nearly got the better of her dread of the monster; but was ready to sink with horror, when he said:

"Beauty, will you be my wife?"

She was afraid of putting him in a passion by refusing, and remained silent for a few moments before saying:

"No, Beast."

The Beast sighed deeply, and said, in a melancholy tone:

"Adieu, Beauty!" and left her, turning his head two or three times as he went, to look at her once more. Beauty, finding herself alone, began to feel the greatest compassion for the poor Beast.

"Alas!" said she, "what a pity it is he should be so very frightful, since he is good-tempered!"

Beauty lived three months in this palace, very contentedly: the Beast visited her every evening, and entertained her with his conversation while she supped, and though what he said was not very clever, yet, perceiving in him every day new virtues, instead of dreading the time of his coming, she continually looked at her watch, to see if it was almost nine o'clock; at which time he never failed to visit her. There was but one thing that made her uneasy; which was that the Beast, before he retired, constantly asked her if she would be his wife, and appeared extremely sorrowful at her refusals. Beauty one day said to him:

"You distress me exceedingly, Beast, in obliging me to refuse you so often: I wish I could prevail on myself to marry you, but I am too sincere to flatter you that this will ever happen."

"I love you exceedingly," replied the Beast; "however,

I think myself fortunate in your being pleased to stay with me; promise me, Beauty, that you will never leave me."

Beauty was quite confused when he said this, for she had seen in her glass that her father had fallen sick of grief for her absence, and pined to see her.

"I would willingly promise," said she, "never to leave you entirely; but I have such a longing desire to see my father, that if you refuse me this pleasure I shall die of grief."

"Rather would I die myself, Beauty," replied he, "than cause you affliction. I will send you to your father's cottage; you shall stay there, and your poor Beast shall die of grief."

"No," said Beauty, weeping, "I love you too well to be the cause of your death: I promise to return in a week; you have shown me that my sisters are married, and my brothers gone to the army; my father is therefore all alone. Allow me to pass one week with him."

"You shall find yourself with him to-morrow morning," answered the Beast, "but remember your promise. When you wish to return you have only to put your ring on a table when you go to bed. Adieu, Beauty!"

The Beast sighed, and Beauty went to bed extremely affected to

see him so distressed. When she awoke in the morning, she found herself in her father's cottage. Ringing a bell that was at her bedside, a servant entered, and on seeing her, gave a loud shriek; upon which the merchant ran upstairs, and, on beholding his daughter, was ready to die of joy. They embraced again and again; at length, Beauty began to recollect that she had no clothes to put on; but the servant told her she had just found a large chest filled with apparel, embroidered all over with gold, and ornamented with pearls and diamonds. Beauty thanked the kind Beast in her thoughts for his attention, and dressed herself in the plainest of the gowns, telling the servant to put away the others carefully, for she intended to present them to her sisters: but scarcely had she pronounced these words than the chest disappeared. Her father then observed, that no doubt the Beast intended she should keep the whole for herself; and immediately the chest returned to the same place.

While Beauty was dressing herself, notice was sent to her sisters of her arrival, and they lost no time in coming with their husbands to pay her a visit The husband of the eldest was extremely handsome; but so vain of his person, that he thought of nothing else from morning till night, and wholly disregarded the beauty of his wife. The second had married a man of excellent understanding; but he made no other use of it than to torment and affront all his acquaintances and his wife. The two sisters were ready to burst with envy when they saw Beauty dressed like a princess, and looking so very beautiful; not all the kindness she showed them produced the least effect; their jealousy was still increased, when she told them how happily she lived at the palace of the Beast. The envious creatures went secretly into the garden, where they cried with spite, to think of her good fortune.

"Sister," said the eldest, "let us try to keep her here beyond the week allowed by the Beast; who will then be so enraged, that ten to one but he eats her up in a moment."

Having determined on this, they joined her in the cottage, and showed her so much affection, that Beauty could not help crying for joy. When the week was ended, the two sisters began to tear their hair, and counterfeited so much affliction at the thoughts of her leaving them, that she consented to stay another week; during which Beauty could not help constantly reproaching herself for the unhappiness she knew she must occasion her poor Beast, whom she tenderly loved, and for whose company she much wished. The tenth night of her being at the cottage, she dreamed she was in the garden of the palace, and that the Beast lay expiring, and in a dying voice reproached her with ingratitude. Beauty awaked and burst into tears.

"Am I not very wicked," said she, "to act so unkindly to a Beast who has treated me with such kindness? It is not his fault that he is ugly and stupid; and then he is so good! which is far better than all the rest. Why do I refuse to marry him? I should certainly be happier with him than my sisters with their husbands, for it is neither the person nor understanding of a husband that makes his wife happy, but kindness, virtue, and obliging temper; and all these the Beast possesses in perfection. I do not love him, but I feel for him the sincerest friendship, esteem, and gratitude."

She put her ring on the table, and soon fell asleep again. In the morning she found herself in the palace of the Beast; dressed herself with great magnificence, that she might please him the better, and thought she had never passed so long a day. At length the clock struck nine, but no Beast appeared. Beauty imagined she had been the cause of his death; she

ran from room to room all over the palace, calling in despair upon his name; but still no Beast came. After seeking for a long time, she recollected her dream, and instantly ran towards the grass plot on which she had seen him; and there she found the poor Beast extended senseless, and to all appearance dead. She threw herself upon his body, thinking nothing at all of his ugliness, and finding his heart still beat, she ran hastily and fetched some water, and threw it on his face. The Beast opened his eyes, and said:

"You forgot your promise, Beauty. My grief for the loss of you made me resolve to starve

57

myself to death; at least I shall die content, since I have had the pleasure of seeing you once more."

" No, dear Beast," replied Beauty, "you shall not die; you shall live to become my husband; from this moment I offer you my hand, and swear to be only yours. Alas! I thought I felt only friendship for you; but the pain I feel convinces me that I could not live without seeing you."

Scarcely had Beauty pronounced these words, before the palace was suddenly illuminated, and music, fireworks, and all kinds of amusements announced the most splendid rejoicings. This, however, had no effect on Beauty, who watched over her dear Beast with the most tender anxiety. But what was her amazement, to see all at once at her feet the handsomest prince that was ever seen, who thanked her with the utmost tenderness for having broken his enchantment! Though this prince was deserving her whole attention, she could not refrain from asking him what was become of the Beast.

" You see him, Beauty, at your feet," answered the prince. " A wicked fairy had condemned me to keep the form of a

beast till a beautiful young lady should consent to marry me,
and had forbidden me on pain of death to show that I had
any understanding. You alone, dearest Beauty, have had the
generosity to judge of me by the goodness of my heart; and,

in offering you my crown, the recompense falls infinitely short
of what I owe you."

Beauty, in the most pleasing surprise, assisted the handsome prince to rise, and they proceeded together to the palace;
when her astonishment was very great, to find there her father
and all her family, who had been conveyed thither by the
beautiful lady she saw in her dream.

"Beauty," said the lady (for she was a great fairy),
"receive the reward of the virtuous choice you have made.
You have preferred goodness of heart to sense and beauty:

you therefore deserve to find these qualities united in the same person. You are going to be a great queen: I hope a crown will not destroy your virtue. As for you, ladies," said the fairy to the eldest sisters, "I have long been witness to the malice of your hearts, and the injustice you have committed. You shall become two statues; but under that form you shall preserve your reason as before, and shall be fixed at the gates of your sister's palace; nor will I inflict on you any greater punishment than that of witnessing her happiness. You will never recover your natural forms till you are fully sensible of your faults; and, to say the truth, I much fear you will ever remain statues. I have sometimes seen that pride, anger, and idleness may be conquered; but to amend a malignant and envious temper would be absolutely a miracle."

At the same instant the fairy, with a stroke of her wand, transported all who were present to the young prince's dominions, where he was received with transports of joy by his subjects. He married Beauty, and passed with her a long and happy life, because their actions were founded upon virtue.

Valentine and Orson

ELLISANT, the beautiful sister of the re-
nowned Pepin, King of France, was married
to Alexander, Emperor of Constantinople.
Now the Emperor's chief minister was the
high priest, a selfish and cruel man, who,
observing the goodness of the new Empress, feared that she might acquire too
much influence in her new country, and so wickedly resolved
to seek her destruction.

The Emperor was a suspicious and credulous man, and
one day when he was alone the High Priest entered the apartment saying:

"May your Majesty be ever guarded from the base
attempts of the wicked and treacherous! I may not, being
a priest, reveal the name of the criminal who has entrusted to
me a dreadful secret; but, in the most solemn manner, I con-
jure your Majesty to beware of the designs of the Empress:

for that beautiful and dissembling lady is faithless and disloyal, and even now is planning your death."

The Emperor, believing the High Priest's tale, could not restrain his fury; but, still loving the Queen, could not bring himself to pronounce the sentence of her execution; yet he resolved to banish her from his dominions, and commanded her to leave Constantinople. At the same time he forbade all persons, on pain of death, to assist or succour the unfortunate lady, allowing her no other attendant than her servant Blandiman, whom she had brought with her from France. Thus with her one faithful attendant she left the city where she had been Empress.

"Alas!" cried she, "now all my happiness is fled. Instead of cloth of gold, I am clad in mean attire; my precious stones of inestimable value are all taken from me, and only pearls of tears adorn my garments. Ah! my brother, what shouldst thou do with such a woeful sister?"

As she was thus complaining and weeping, her servant said to her:

"Alas! be not discomforted, but trust in Providence, who will keep and defend you!"

Having thus spoken, he espied a fountain, towards which they took their way. After refreshing themselves they proceeded towards France. Arriving at the forest of Orleans, the disconsolate princess was so overcome with grief and fatigue, that she was unable to proceed farther. Her faithful attendant gathered fallen leaves and moss to make a couch for her, and then hastened away to seek some habitation where he might procure food and assistance.

During Blandiman's absence the royal lady became the mother of two beautiful sons. She pressed the lovely infants by turns to her bosom, and shed tears of joy over them; when suddenly a huge bear rushed upon her, and snatching up one of the babes in its mouth, hastened into the thickest part of the forest. The wretched mother, distracted at the fate of her child, pursued the bear with shrieks and lamentations; till overcome with anguish and terror, she fell into a swoon near the mouth of the cave into which the bear had borne her infant. It happened that King Pepin, accompanied by several great lords and barons of the court, was on that day hunting in the forest of Orleans, and chanced to pass near the tree where the son of Bellisant lay sleeping on its bed of moss. The King was astonished with the beauty of the child, who opened his eyes as the King stood gazing on him, and, smiling, stretched out its little arms.

"See," said King Pepin, "this lovely infant seems to solicit my favour."

The King little imagined it was his nephew, the son of his sister Bellisant, that he now delivered into the hands of one of his pages, who took the babe to Orleans to be nursed, and gave it, by the King's orders, the name of Valentine. Scarcely had the page ridden away with the child, than the King met Blandiman, and demanded with great surprise what news from Constantinople. Blandiman, bending one knee to the ground, began to relate the disasters of the Empress; but upon King Pepin's hearing that the High Priest had accused her of plotting the Emperor's death, he flew into the most violent rage against his innocent sister, and said:

"I cannot believe the loyal High Priest would bring a false accusation against anyone, and I blame the Emperor for sparing the life of his treacherous, disloyal Queen: but let her beware how she comes into my power; and hear me, nobles,

henceforth it is death for anyone that names her in my presence."

So saying, he proceeded towards Orleans. Blandiman, with a heavy heart, searched the forest for his injured mistress, and at length espied her on the ground tearing her hair, and uttering cries of grief.

"Ah! Blandiman," she exclaimed, "but an hour since I was the joyful mother of two beautiful babes. A ravenous bear snatched one, and some other cruel beast of prey has doubtless devoured the other. At the foot of yonder tree I left it when I pursued the bear; but no trace of either of my children remains. They are gone, gone for ever; and I, wretched mother, have nothing left but to die. Go, Blandiman, leave me to perish, and tell the mighty Emperor of Constantinople to what a horrible fate he has destined his innocent wife and children."

Blandiman would not leave the unfortunate Queen; and when she became more calm, prevailed on her to take shelter in a monastery on the borders of the forest of Orleans. After some time he told her of the unjust wrath of King Pepin against her; which renewed the sorrows of the hapless lady, and determined her to continue in the monastery.

The bear that had carried away the infant, bore it to her cave, and laid it down unhurt before her young ones. The cubs, however, did not devour it, but stroked it with their rough paws: and the old bear perceiving their kindness for the little babe, gave it suck, and nourished it in this manner for the space of a whole year. The child became hardy and robust, and as it grew in strength, began to range the forest, and attack the wild beasts with such fury, that they shunned the cave where he continued to live with the old bear. He passed this kind of life during eighteen years, until he was the terror of the neighbouring country. The name of Orson was given to him, because he was nurtured by a bear; and his renown spread over all France. King Pepin had a great desire to see the wild man of the woods; and one day rode with his retinue into the forest of Orleans, in hopes of meeting him. The King, leaving his train at some distance, rode on, and passed near the cave which Orson inhabited. On hearing the sound of horses' feet, the wild man rushed upon the King, and would have strangled him in an instant, but for a valiant knight, who galloped up and wounded Orson with his sword. Orson then left the King, and running furiously upon the knight, caught him and his horse, and overthrew both. The King, being quite unarmed, could not assist the knight, but rode away to call the attendants to his rescue. However, before they arrived on the spot, the unfortunate knight was torn to pieces, and Orson had fled to the thickest part of the forest, where all their endeavours could not discover him. The noise of this adventure increased everyone's terror, and the neighbouring villages were nearly abandoned by their inhabitants.

Valentine, in the meanwhile, had been educated in all kinds of accomplishments, with the King's fair daughter, Eglantine. Nothing could exceed the fondness of the young people for each other: indeed, there never was a lovelier princess than Eglantine, or a braver and more accomplished knight than Valentine. Valentine soon distinguished himself above the other leaders in battle. He fought near the King's side; and when his Majesty was taken by a troop of Saracens, Valentine rushed through their ranks, slew hundreds of them, and replacing the King on his horse, led him off in triumph.

Valentine having conquered the pagans, returned to the court of King Pepin, and was received with loud acclamations by the people, and joyfully welcomed by the Princess Eglantine. The distinctions and favour showered on him raised the envy and hatred of Henry and Haufray, the King's sons.

It happened shortly after that a petition was presented to the King, praying relief against Orson, the wild man of the woods; the fear of whom was now become so great that the peasants dared not go out to till their fields, nor the shepherds to watch their flocks. The King issued a proclamation, saying, that if any man would undertake to bring Orson,

dead or alive, to the city, he should receive a thousand marks of gold.

"Sire," said Henry, "I think no person is so proper to undertake this enterprise as the foundling Valentine, on whom your Majesty lavishes such great favours. Perhaps if he conquers the naked savage with his sword, you will not think it too much to reward him with the hand of our sister Eglantine."

Valentine fixing a firm look on the malicious brother, said:

"You give this counsel to compass my death: be it so. Know that I will not fail of victory here also. I will go without delay, and alone, to conquer the savage man."

"No, Valentine," said the King, "you shall not rush into destruction to gratify the ill will of evil-minded persons."

"Pardon me, my liege," replied Valentine; "it concerns my honour that I go. I will encounter this danger, and every other, rather than not prove myself worthy of your Majesty's favour and protection. To-morrow I will depart for the forest at the break of day."

At dawn, Valentine arose; and putting on his armour, having his shield polished like a mirror, he departed; and being arrived at the forest he alighted, and tying his horse to

a tree, penetrated into the thickest part of the wood in search of Orson. He long wandered in vain, and being come near the mouth of a large cave, thought that might be the hiding-place of the wild man. Valentine then climbed a high tree near the cave: and scarcely was he seated among the branches than he heard Orson's roar. Orson had been hunting, and came with a swift pace, bearing a buck he had killed upon his shoulders. Valentine could not help admiring the beauty of his person, the grace and freedom of his motions, and his appearance of strength and agility. He felt a species of affection for the wild man, and wished it were possible to tame him. Valentine tore off a branch of the tree; and threw it at Orson's feet, who, looking up, and espying him in the tree, uttered a growl of fury, and darted up the tree like lightning. Valentine quickly descended on the other side. Orson seeing him on the ground, leaped down, and opening his arms, prepared in his usual manner, to rush upon and overthrow his antagonist; but Valentine, holding up the polished steel, Orson suddenly beheld, instead of the person he meant to seize, his own wild figure. Upon Valentine's lowering the shield, he again saw his enemy, and with a cry of transport again prepared to grasp him in his arms. The strength of Orson was so very great, that Valentine was unable to defend himself without having recourse to his sword. When Orson received a wound from his sword, he uttered loud shrieks of anger and surprise, and instantly tearing up by the roots a large tree, furiously attacked Valentine. A dreadful fight now ensued between these two brothers, and the victory was for a long time doubtful: Orson receiving many dreadful wounds from the sword of Valentine, and Valentine with great difficulty escaping from being crushed to death beneath the weighty club of Orson. Just at this time, the bear who had nursed Orson, and who was now in the cave, hearing the cries of rage, came out to see what was the matter with her favourite. Valentine, perceiving her approach, aimed a blow at her with his sword, which would probably have killed her on the spot, had not Orson rushed forward; and throwing one arm round the neck of the bear, he with the other hand supplicated for mercy for his old and only friend. Valentine was greatly affected with this generous action, and, laying aside his sword, made signs that he would not hurt the bear, and, in token of kindness, brought some grapes and a bottle of wine he had deposited near for his own refreshment in case of need, and presented them to Orson.

Orson no sooner tasted the flavour of the fruit than he gave it to the bear, and afterwards let her drink the wine, with both of which she seemed much pleased; while Orson, delighted to see her make such a repast, threw his arms round her and embraced her; and the bear, desirous to gratify her affection for him, stroked him with her huge paw, and uttered a gentle growl, as if to express her satisfaction.

Valentine now made many signs to Orson, persuading him to go with him, where he should be fed and clothed, and treated with the greatest kindness; but

Orson rejected all his offers with anger and contempt, making signs that he never would quit his beloved bear, nor his wild life in the woods. But it happened that the wine which the bear had drunk so greedily from Valentine's bottle caused her death; and soon after, testifying her love for Orson in the manner we have described, she faintly howled, and fell dead on the ground. Orson stood for a few moments motionless with alarm and amazement; then supposing his ancient friend might be only asleep, he stooped and endeavoured to rouse her, but finding all his efforts ineffectual, his grief is scarcely to be described. He threw himself upon the body, and uttered piercing shrieks of distress. At length he suddenly sprang up from the ground, and approaching Valentine made signs that he would now be his; and while the tears ran down his cheeks for the loss of his bear, he suffered Valentine to bind his hands, and followed his conductor. Valentine took his way towards Orleans; but wherever he passed, the people, perceiving the wild man, ran into their houses and hid themselves. On arriving at an inn where Valentine intended resting during the night, the terrified inhabitants fastened the door, and would not suffer them to enter. Valentine made signs to Orson, who, placing his shoulder against the door, forced it open in an instant, upon which the people of the inn all ran out at the back, and would not venture to return. A great feast was in preparation, and there was plenty of fowls and good provisions roasting at the fire. Orson tore the meat off the spit with his hands, and devoured it greedily; and espying a cauldron of water, put his head into it, and drank like a horse.

In the morning, Valentine resumed his journey, leading Orson as before. On arriving at the city, the inhabitants shut their doors, and ran into the highest rooms to gaze upon the wild man. Being come to the outer court of King Pepin's palace, the porter in a great fright barred the gate with heavy chains and bars of iron, and could not be prevailed upon to open it. After soliciting admittance for some time, and being still denied, Valentine made a sign to Orson, who, tearing up one of the large stone posts that stood by, shattered the gate to pieces. The Queen, the Princess Eglantine, and all their attendants, fled to hide themselves when they heard that Orson was arrived; and Valentine had the greatest difficulty in persuading them to believe that Orson was no longer furious and savage as he had been in the woods. At length the King permitted him to be brought in; and the whole court gathered in the apartment, and were much amused by his wild actions and gestures, although very cautious not to come near him. On Valentine's making signs, he kissed the King's robe, and the hand of the Princess Eglantine; for Orson had now become so attached to Valentine that he would obey him in all things, and would suffer no other person to control him.

Very soon after the capture of Orson, a herald appeared at the court of King Pepin, from the Duke of Aquitaine, summoning all true knights to avenge the cause of the Lady Fezon, daughter to the noble duke who was held in cruel captivity by Agramont, the Green Knight: the herald proclaiming, that whoever should conquer the Green Knight should receive the hand of the Lady Fezon in marriage, together with a princely dowry. This Green Knight was so famous for his cruelty and his victories, that the young lords of the court all drew back, and seemed unwilling to enter the lists; for it was known that he was defended by enchantment, and it was his practice to hang upon a high tree all the knights whom he had defeated. Valentine, however, offered himself without hesitation, and engaged to get ready and depart the next morning. The Princess Eglantine secretly resolved, if possible, to prevent the destruction of her beloved Valentine, by combating the Green Knight herself. She contrived to steal away the armour of Valentine while he slept, and equipping herself in it, mounted a fiery courser; and attended only by her favourite maid, in quality of a page, proceeded to the castle which the Green Knight inhabited, and where he kept the Lady Fezon a prisoner.

Valentine, meanwhile, missing his armour when he arose, and learning that the Princess had taken it and was gone on the perilous enterprise, was almost distracted with terrors for her safety. He ordered his horse to be prepared, and, followed by Orson, set out in search of the Princess. Haufray and Henry, disappointed in their former purpose, now resolved to waylay and kill Valentine. Accordingly, in a narrow alley of a dark wood, they sprang upon him, and seized him before he had power to draw his sword. Orson chanced to be a little way behind, but, upon hearing Valentine's voice, he rushed upon Henry who was about to stab Valentine in the back, and seized him in his arms. Orson's grasp almost crushed Henry to death, and Valentine would have killed Haufray, but first tearing their masks from their faces, and seeing they were the King's sons, he left them to the shame and disgrace their base conduct would bring upon them. He had some difficulty in prevailing on Orson to let them live; but they left the wicked brothers in the wood, and continued their journey, fortunately arriving at the castle of the Green Knight, just as the Princess Eglantine was almost overpowered in the combat. Valentine rushed with dreadful fury upon the Green Knight, and the fight was long and equal. At length Agramont demanded a parley.

"Knight," said he to Valentine, "thou art brave and noble. Behold; yonder hang twenty knights whom I have subdued and executed: such will be thy fate; I give thee warning."

"Base traitor," replied Valentine, "I fear thee not; come on; I defy thee."

"First," rejoined the Green Knight, "fetch me yonder shield; for in pity to thy youth, I tell thee, unless thou canst remove that shield, thou never canst rescue the Lady Fezon, or conquer me."

Valentine approached the shield; but, in spite of all his efforts, he could not loosen it from the tree, though it appeared to hang but on a slender branch. Valentine, breathless with his exertions to pull down the shield, stood leaning against the tree, when Agramont with a loud laugh exclaimed:

"Fly and save thyself, fair knight; for since thou canst not move the shield, thou art not destined to be my victor. Further, know, there is no one living who can subdue me, unless he be the son of a mighty king, and yet was suckled by a wild beast."

Valentine started on hearing these latter words, and ran

to Orson, who had been all this time employed in gazing with looks of delight and admiration on the Lady Fezon. Valentine led him to the enchanted shield, which, on Orson's raising his arm towards it, dropped instantly from its place. The Green Knight trembled and turned pale; then, gnashing his teeth, seized his sword, and attacked Orson with desperate fury. At the first blow, Agramont's trusty sword broke in pieces upon the enchanted shield. Next he caught up a battleaxe, which snapped instantly in two. He then called for a lance, which shivered to atoms in the same manner. Furious with these defeats, he threw aside his weapons, and trusting to his wonderful strength, attempted to grasp Orson in his arms; but Orson, seizing him as if he had been a mere child dashed him on the ground, and would have instantly

destroyed him, had not Valentine interposed to save his life. Orson continued to hold him down till some chains were brought, when, in despite of the furious struggles of the Green Knight, Orson bound him in strong fetters, to lead him away a prisoner.

Agramont addressed himself to Valentine, and said:

"This savage man is my conqueror; therefore there must be some mystery in his fate. Haste, then, to the castle of my brother Ferragus, where you will find a Brazen Head that will explain to you who he is."

Valentine, having dispatched a herald to acquaint the Duke of Aquitaine with the release of his daughter, sent the Lady Fezon, with the Princess Eglantine, to the court of King Pepin, while he and Orson proceeded to the castle of the giant Ferragus. This castle was guarded by two lions, who roared with rage against Valentine, but when Orson appeared, they lay down and crouched beneath his feet. On entering the castle, a dwarf approached, and conducted them to a chamber abounding with gold, rubies, and other precious stones; in the centre there were four pillars of jasper, two of which were as yellow as the finest gold, a third more green than grass, and a fourth more red than a flame of fire. Between these pillars was an emerald of amazing value; and in the midst the Brazen Head rested upon a rich pedestal. Before the pedestal stood an enormous giant, who lifted his club to forbid their approach, but Orson seized him by the middle, and bore him from the chamber to a dungeon, where he secured him. Valentine fixed his eyes upon the Brazen Head, anxious to hear what it would say concerning his birth. At length when Orson had returned it spake thus:

"Thou, O renowned knight, art called Valentine the brave, and art the man destined to be the husband of the Princess Eglantine of France. Thou art son to the Emperor of Greece, and thy mother is Bellisant, sister to King Pepin of France. She was unjustly banished from her throne, and took refuge in a monastery, where she has resided these twenty years. The wild man, who hath so long accompanied thee, is thy brother. You were both born in the forest of Orleans.

Thou wert found and brought up under the care of King Pepin thy uncle, but thy brother was stolen and nurtured by a bear. Proceed, Valentine, to France, where thou wilt find the innocent Empress, thy hapless mother; at the moment when she embraces thy brother, speech will be given to him. Away, and prosper! These are the last words I shall utter. Fate has decreed that, when Valentine and Orson enter this chamber my power ends."

Having thus spoken, the Brazen Head fell from its pedestal: thunder shook the foundations of the castle; they were surrounded with thick darkness; and when the light again burst upon them, they found themselves on an open plain, and no traces of the castle remained. The little dwarf, whose name was Pacolet, at the same time appeared before them on a winged horse and said:

"Noble youths, I go before you to the court of King Pepin, to prepare your royal parents, who are already there, for your reception."

And instantly Pacolet mounted into the air, and was presently out of sight. Valentine now fell upon the bosom of his brother Orson, and Orson upon his; they embraced each other with the utmost affection, and joyfully proceeded towards France. While these transactions were passing, the Emperor of Constantinople had lived in great affliction for the loss of his Queen. The wicked High Priest had continued to represent her as the vilest of women, and to abuse the Emperor's confidence in him till he was on his deathbed; when, repenting of his treachery, he sent for the Emperor, and confessed before the whole court that he had basely slandered the princess. Nothing could exceed the Emperor's grief. He immediately set out with all his nobles for France, to implore King Pepin to assist him in searching for Bellisant. In every town on his journey he caused her innocence to be proclaimed, and offered an immense reward to anyone who should bring tidings of her to the court of King Pepin. It happened that Blandiman, who was buying provisions for the monastery at Orleans, as the Emperor passed through, heard the proclamation, and hastened with the tidings to his mistress. The Empress, overjoyed to have her innocence made known, quitted the monastery, and went to the palace of her brother, where she was received with shouts of triumph—King Pepin and the Emperor both falling at her feet to implore forgiveness. Scarcely had the reconciliation passed, and the Empress related her sorrowful history when the dwarf, Pacolet, appeared on the winged horse, to announce the wonderful declaration made by the Brazen Head, and the approach of

the royal brothers. The noble youths now presented themselves to their parents; and no sooner had the Empress Bellisant thrown her arms round the neck of her son Orson, than speech was given to him, and he expressed his duty and affection to his parents and uncle, in terms of such grace and propriety, as at once astonished and delighted the whole court. The Duke of Aquitaine, having already come to the palace of King Pepin, to congratulate his daughter, now took the hand of Orson, and presented him to the Lady Fezon as her future husband: King Pepin at the same time joined the hands of Valentine and the Princess Eglantine. Splendid preparations were immediately made for the celebration of the nuptials; and for a whole month nothing was to be heard of throughout France but tilts and tournaments, feasts and balls, fireworks and illuminations, with every other kind of splendid and magnificent entertainment.

Little Red Riding Hood

NCE upon a time there lived a country girl, who was the sweetest little creature ever seen. Her grandmother had made for her a pretty red hood, which so became the child that everyone called her Little Red Riding-Hood. One day her mother, having made some cakes, said to her:

"Go, my child, and see how your grandmother does, for I hear she is ill; carry her some of these cakes, and a little pot of butter."

Little Red Riding-Hood, with a basket filled with the

cakes and the pot of butter, immediately set out for her grandmother's house, in a village a little distance away.

As she was crossing a wood she met a wolf, who had a mind to eat her up, but dared not do so because of some woodcutters at work near them in the forest. He ventured, however, to ask her whither she was going.

The little girl, not knowing how dangerous it was to talk to a wolf, replied:

"I am going to see my grandmother, and carry her these cakes and a pot of butter."

"Does she live far off?" said the wolf.

"Oh, yes," answered Little Red Riding-Hood, "beyond the mill you see yonder, at the first house in the village."

"Well," said the wolf, "I will go and see her too; I will take this way and you take that, and see which will be there the soonest."

The wolf set out, running as fast as he could, and taking the nearest way, while the little girl took the longest, and amused herself as she went along with gathering nuts, running after butterflies, and making nosegays of such flowers as she found within her reach.

The wolf soon arrived at the grandmother's cottage, and knocked at the door.

"Who is there?" asked a voice.

"It is your grandchild, Little Red Riding-Hood," said the wolf, counterfeiting her voice; "I have brought you some cakes and a little pot of butter, which Mother has sent you."

The good old woman, who was ill in bed, called out:

"Pull the bobbin, and the latch will go up."

The wolf pulled the bobbin, and the door opened. He sprang upon the poor old grandmother and ate her up in a moment.

The wolf then shut the door and laid himself down in the bed, and waited for Little Red Riding-Hood, who arrived soon after. Tap! Tap!

"Who is there?"

She was at first a little frightened at the hoarse voice of the wolf, but supposing that her grandmother had got a cold, answered:

"It is your grandchild, Little Red Riding-Hood. Mother has sent you some cakes and a little pot of butter." The wolf called out, softening his voice:

"Pull the bobbin, and the latch will go up."

Little Red Riding-Hood pulled the bobbin, and the door opened.

When she came into the room, the wolf, hiding himself under the bedclothes, said, trying all he could to speak in a feeble voice:

"Put the basket, my child, on the stool; take off your clothes, and come into bed with me."

The Wolf arrives at the Cottage

LITTLE RED RIDING-HOOD

Little Red Riding-Hood accordingly undressed herself and stepped into bed, where, wondering to see how her grandmother looked in her nightclothes, she said:

"Grandmother, what great arms you have got."

"The better to hug thee, my child."

"Grandmother, what great ears you have got."

"The better to hear thee, my child."

"Grandmother, what great eyes you have got."

"The better to see thee, my child."

"Grandmother, what great teeth you have got."

"The better to eat thee up;" and saying these words, the wicked wolf fell upon poor Little Red Riding-Hood, and ate her up in a few mouthfuls.